Anonymous

A Scriptural Refutation of a Pamphlet

Anonymous

A Scriptural Refutation of a Pamphlet

ISBN/EAN: 9783744794220

Printed in Europe, USA, Canada, Australia, Japan

Cover: Foto ©ninafisch / pixelio.de

More available books at **www.hansebooks.com**

A

SCRIPTURAL REFUTATION

OF A

PAMPHLET,

LATELY PUBLISHED BY THE REV. RAYMUND HARRIS,

INTITLED,

"SCRIPTURAL RESEARCHES

ON THE

LICITNESS OF THE SLAVE TRADE."

In FOUR LETTERS from the AUTHOR
to a FRIEND.

THE SECOND EDITION.

————" from love of grace
Lay not *his flattering unction* to your fouls."

LONDON:

PRINTED AND SOLD BY J. PHILLIPS, GEORGE-YARD,
LOMBARD-STREET.
MDCCLXXXVIII.

A

Scriptural Refutation, &c.

L E T T E R I.

I HAVE perufed with fome degree of attention, the very extraordinary pamphlet which
you lately fent me, intitled, " *Scriptural Refearches
on the* LICITNESS *of the Slave Trade, by the Rev.
Raymund Harris;*" in which the author has endeavoured to fhew " *its conformity with the principles
of natural and revealed religion, as delineated in the
facred writings of the word of God.*"
Although I have not that high opinion of the
ftate of improvement, in this age and country,
which many perfons profefs to entertain, yet I own
I could not avoid being furprifed, that either the
one or the other, fhould have been infulted by
the publication of a work, which, if its dangerous
and deftructive principles were admitted in their
full extent, would fhake the foundations of fociety, and eftablifh, *by the fanction of divine autho-*

rity,

rity, every variety of oppreffion, and every fpecies of guilt.

The fhort account you gave me of the character and profeffion of the author, operated however as a fort of comment on his work. The unnatural attachment to flavery—the averfion and dread of the interference of reafon and common fenfe—the artful and fubtle pofitions which are the foundation of his work, appear totally irreconcileable to the character of an *Englifhman*, but are perfectly confiftent with that of *a Spanifh Jefuit*.

I muft not, however, charge the Rev. Raymund Harris with being the firft who has openly attempted the juftification of moral guilt from the books of the Old and New Teftament. So long ago as the beginning of the 15th century, one *John Petit*, a doctor of the church in France, not only publickly juftified the murder of the Duke of Orleans, by the Duke of Burgundy, but took occafion, at the fame time, to affert the *general legality* (or, as it is now expreffed, the *licitnefs*) of homicide, which he founded on the example of all the murders mentioned in the Old Teftament, by making that *a rule of conduct*, which was only introduced as *a mere hiftorical narrative*.

As I have at prefent a little leifure, I think I cannot employ it to better purpofe, than in ftripping the mafk from this concealed enemy of order and religion, and expofing him to the world in his proper colours. But before I enter on the examination of his work, it may not be improper to premife, that I fhall confine myfelf to the mode of proof he has himfelf prefcribed; viz. *to that derived from the authority of the facred writings only—* not thinking it in any degree neceffary in the refutation

futation of his work, to refort to thofe more general arguments which are derived from the nature of man, and the univerfal principles of truth
and juftice, as implanted in the human mind, by
the immediate hand of its great Author; nor
availing myfelf of an objection, which might be
reafonably made, viz. That in difcuffing a matter
of right between the Europeans and the Africans,
an appeal is made to an authority, which one of
the parties only acknowledge as legitimate.

But though I fhall confine myfelf to the proofs
and authorities deduced from the facred writings,
yet I cannot fo far coincide with Mr. H's wifh, as
entirely to diveft myfelf of " *the fcanty light of mere
human reafon and fenfe,*" which, notwithftanding
the opprobium thrown upon it by Mr. H. in his
preface, I cannot help thinking, is in fome degree neceffary, to enable us to underftand thofe
writings. Mr. H. indeed afterwards informs us,
that he has prefixed to the whole of his work, a few
pofitions or data, which he trufts will be found
unqueftionably true, and *exactly conformable to
found reafon;* and thus, whilft in one breath he
impeaches the authority of this ultimate judge of
truth, in the next he admits it to queftion his
firft principles.

With this permiffion then, I fhall, in the prefent letter, take the liberty of ftating a few of his
data (which are twelve in number), and trying
whether they are confiftent with found reafon or
not; in which I fhall endeavour to be as concife
as the nature of the fubject will admit.

His 1ft and 2d pofitions are,

" *That*

" That the volume of the sacred writings,
" commonly called the Holy Bible, compre-
" hending both the Old and New Testa-
" ments, contains the unerring decisions of
" the word of God. That these decisions are
" of equal authority in both the Testaments;
" and that that authority is the essential ve-
" racity of God, who is truth itself."

Now if we for a moment apply to these positions the touchstone of human reason, we shall
find that some of them are fundamentally false;
and that all of them are to be understood with
many restrictions and exceptions. That the Old
and New Testaments contain the unerring decisions of God, where God has expressly given them
to us as his decisions, every Christian will readily
admit; but it is obvious, that the far greater part
of the Old and New Testaments, consist, not of
decisions, but *of mere historical facts,* some of them
affording instances of a virtuous, and others of a
vicious conduct. That other parts of the scriptures, even where such decisions are found, are
not of general use, but are applicable only to
particular times, or to a particular people. That *it is not*
true that the decisions of the Old and New Testaments are of equal authority, for that the former
is always controlled by the latter; which has totally abrogated many parts of the Mosaic law,
and made an essential difference, not only in the
ritual, but in the moral duties enjoined by the
Old Testament, as I shall hereafter have occasion
to shew more at large.

The

The essence of his four next positions is, *That whatever is declared to be right or wrong in the scriptures, is so in its nature, and cannot be questioned without great presumption; but must be assented to without reserve, however contrary it may be to the opinions of men for any length of time.* But these positions are also laid down in a form, much too general to be admitted by the professors of any religion, except that in which the reverend author was educated. It will readily be granted, that whenever the scriptures have decided on general principles of right and wrong, such decisions are unerring; but it must also be granted, that when those decisions have a reference to the situation of a particular person, or a particular nation, they ought not to be arbitrarily and indiscriminately applied to other persons, or other nations: And if from the powers given to the Jews over their enemies, the permission of certain acts in particular cases, and the existence of certain customs amongst them, we were to infer a right in ourselves, to imitate their actions, and practise their customs, whenever we thought there was a similarity in our situation, the book of the Old Testament might be converted into a *general voucher* for the *licitness* of almost every crime, and every enormity, whether national or individual.

Mr. H. proceeds in his 5th datum to state, " *That if one or more decisions of the* " *written word of God give a positive sanc-* " *tion to the intrinsic licitness of any human* " *pursuit, for instance, the Slave Trade, who-* " *ever professes to believe the incontrovert-* " *ible veracity of the written word of God*

A 4 " *essentially*

" *essentially incompatible with the leaft degree*
" *of injuftice, muft confequently believe the*
" *purfuit itfelf to be intrinfically juft and*
" *lawful in the ftrictest fenfe of the word.*"

From this pofition then it would feem that all
actions which have, under the Jewifh difpenfation,
been practifed by the fanction of divine authority,
are intrinfically and univerfally right, and may
be practifed by all mankind, in all future times,
not only without guilt, but with the ftricteft virtue and propriety; and this moft extenfive rule
is founded on a prefumption, that what God has,
on one occafion, declared to be right, muft alfo
be right on all other occafions, without any attention to the particular circumftances of each.
Suppofing this pofition to be once granted, it is
doubtful whether the depravity of man could commit a crime for which Mr. H. would not, from
the facred writings, extract a better apology than
he has already done for the Slave Trade.   Thus,
for inftance, if any man doubted of the inherent
licitnefs of

I   N   C   E   S   T,

It would be eafy for Mr. Harris to point out the
examples of the daughters of Lot, who each of
them conceived by their father;* which tranf-
action, fo far from being reprefented as criminal,
not only paffes free from the leaft fhadow of re-
prehenfion, but the offspring of this intercourfe,

* Gen. c. xix. v. 30.

became the founders of two powerful nations. Jacob's marrying two fifters,* by each of whom he had children, and who purchafed of each other his favours,† would be an exprefs authority. Were a doubt ftill entertained of the licitnefs of the crime, Mr. H. might refer to the general laws of the Jews, by which the furviving brother was commanded to go in unto his brother's wife, and marry her, and raife up feed to his brother; and might point out an inftance where a refufal to comply with this injunction, brought down upon the offender the immediate vengeance of God.‡ Mr. H. might then advert to the ftate of mankind in the firft age of the world, when the commiffion of this crime was not only excufable, but indifpenfably neceffary to the prefervation of the fpecies; and thus the inherent licitnefs of this heinous offence would be much more fatisfactorily proved than the lawful nature of the African Slave Trade, notwithftanding the indefatigable labour which Mr. H. has beftowed upon it.

F R A U D.

Should any perfon entertain fcruples of confcience, with refpect to the lawfulnefs of defrauding his neighbour, let him adopt Mr. H's pofition, and open the Old Teftament. He will there find that the patriarch Jacob, the immediate founder and ftock of the Jewifh nation, under pretence of a purchafe, defrauded his brother Efau

---

* Gen. chap. xxix. † Gen. chap. xxx. ver. 15.
‡ Gen. chap. xxxviii. v. 8.

of

of his birth-right;* and in order to complete this first piece of treachery, was induced, by a contrivance of the most artful nature, to obtain from his father Isaac, the blessing of the first-born, to the wrong and prejudice of his elder brother. Should he still remain doubtful, he may turn to another incident in the life of the same patriarch, related at large Gen. ch. xxx. ver. 25. in which he will find a stratagem put in execution by Jacob to defraud Laban, his father-in-law, which, according to his position, will justify the inherent licitness of cheating beyond the shadow of contradiction. To these authentic facts, which were the foundation of Jacob's greatness, he may add the authorities that may be deduced from Exod. ch. xi. ver. 2. and ch. xii. ver. 35. where the Israelites abused the confidence of the Egyptians, and deprived them of their jewels, by an express command of their great lawgiver; and the evident conclusion of his *Scriptural Researches on the licitness of fraud* will be, that every man has an inherent right, by the express sanction of the holy scriptures, to defraud his neighbour; nay, *even his brother or his father*, as often as it lies in his power.

It would thus be practicable, under the sanction of Mr. H's 7th position, to select, from the books of the Old Testament, the most evident and incontestable authorities, not only for the lawfulness of lying, theft, polygamy, and fornication, but of the more atrocious crimes of murder, adultery, and revenge; but it is irksome to proceed further under the guidance of *so detestable a proposition*, which, under a pretence of paying an

* Gen. ch. xxv. ver. 29.

implicit

implicit deference to the judgments of God, excludes every confideration of a collateral nature, and thereby renders unjuft and criminal in its general application, that which in the particular inftance, and under peculiar circumftances, was right and lawful, and calls in the authority of the word of God to juftify the commiffion of crimes of the deepeft dye.

The remainder of the author's data are employed to ftate in various lights, *that if any act (e. g. the Slave Trade) be abftractedly and effentially lawful, no abufe or mal-practice can render the principle of it criminal; and that no arguments built folely on thofe abufes can have any weight, unlefs the fame be proved effentially unjuft and illicit.*

To attempt a diftinction between the abftract nature of any thing and the effects produced by it, is well worthy one of the difciples of Loyola; but though thefe fubtleties might have paffed current in the days of our anceftors, they are now fomewhat out of feafon. A fort of maxim has prevailed, that it is improper to reafon from the abufe of any given fubject, againft the ufe of it; but it will furely be granted, that a pronenefs to abufe is itfelf ftrong evidence that fomething is wrong in the principle. It was not by fubtle diftinctions of this kind that our Saviour inftructed his followers: He taught us to judge of the caufe by its effects, and not to fuppofe that could be right in its principle, which was manifeftly wrong in its confequences.—" *A good tree, fays he, cannot bring forth evil fruit, neither can a corrupt tree bring forth good fruit; wherefore by their fruits ye fhall know them,* Matt. chap. vii. ver. 18, 20. What have been the fruits of the African Slave

Trade

Trade I leave to the determination of Mr. H. who, by declining to fubmit to this teft, fhews pretty clearly the fenfe he entertains of the caufe he has undertaken to defend.

From thefe remarks I truft it will evidently appear, that although the fcriptures contain the written will of God, yet, as in reading the facred volumes we muft ufe our eyes, fo, in underftanding them, we muft make ufe of our reafon. It is true, the Church of Rome prohibits its followers not only from confidering, but perufing the fcriptures; and requires them to be implicitly acknowledged as equally and invariably true in all parts. But the Proteftant Churches have difcarded thefe narrow reftraints, and not only permit, but require us to examine the fcriptures with the utmoft degree of attention and care. Shall we then fo far fuffer ourfelves to be blinded by the propofitions, or by the fubfequent denunciations of Mr. H. as to give up at his fimple requeft, a right for which our anceftors ftruggled at the expenfe of their blood? Or fhall we not rather, like men and Proteftants, judge for ourfelves of the fpirit and tendency of the holy fcriptures? Under this idea it will then be neceffary, before we ground our conduct upon the precepts or examples they afford us, diligently to examine whether fuch examples and precepts are *of general and univerfal import*, or only confined to a particular perfon or people. Whether fome things, which are allowed or commanded in the Old Teftament, *be not annulled or explained in the New*, and conftantly to make the moft accurate diftinction between fuch paffages as ought to influence our conduct, and *fuch as are merely narrative*. By thefe means we fhall perceive,

ceive, that it would be as abfurd to affert that the inhabitants of Great Britain can be juftified in carrying away the natives of Africa from their country and friends to perpetual fervitude, *becaufe* the Jews had domeftic flaves in their houfes, as to fuppofe that we have a right to deftroy all the nations round us, *becaufe* Jofhua fmote thirty-one kings on the other fide of the River Jordan.*

* Jofhua, chap. xii. ver. 7.

LETTER

L E T T E R II.

I HAVE in my former letter shewn, that the *data* required by Mr. H. are such as cannot be granted, without confiderable reftrictions upon their import, by any perfon who affumes the character of a Proteftant, or profeffes to make ufe of his reafon in the examination of the fcriptures. In the prefent, I fhall point out in what manner his fubfequent arguments in favour of the Slave Trade, are affected by this correction of his firft principles.

Having ftated as a pofition, that every thing contained in the fcriptures is equally true, and univerfally applicable; without any exception whatever of *perfon*, *time*, or *place*, or the confideration of *any concurring circumftance*, he proceeds to fhew, that the cuftom of flavery was permitted in the ancient world, and cites the particular examples of Abraham, Jofeph, and Jofhua, with many texts on the fubjects; occupying the greateft part of his pamphlet with demonftrating, what no one ever thought of denying, viz. *that the Jews were allowed to purchafe bond-men and bond-women of the Heathen;* and under certain ftipulations to

retain

retain in their service, even those of their own country.

But it is surely somewhat extraordinary, that so acute a Logician, after having at such length laid down his premises, and sanctioned them by such numerous appeals to holy writ, should be *so miserably defective* in drawing his conclusions from them. After having shewn the *licitness* of Slavery to the Jews and their immediate anceftors, it might have been expected, that the author would thence have deduced *the right of the Europeans to enslave the inhabitants of Africa*; but on this important head he is totally silent: and the whole of his reasonings, and researches, are equally calculated to prove, *that the negroes have an inherent right to take us and our families, and carry us into perpetual slavery*, as that we have *a right to pursue the African Slave Trade*.

That the Israelites had the permission of the Divine Being, to retain in their service bondmen and bond-women of the Heathen, and even of their own nation, for a limited time, is granted; but this permission appears to have been particularly confined to that nation, and was not extended to the rest of mankind: Nor is there in Mr. H's researches, the least ground to conclude, that any particular nation succeeded to that extraordinary privilege over other nations, which was exercised by, and allowed to the children of Israel.*

---

* That the practice of *Man-stealing*, as the object of a general law, was considered, both under the old and new dispensation, as a crime of the highest magnitude, may appear from Exodus ch. xxi. ver. 16. Paul's 1st Epistle to Tim. ch. i. ver. 9 and 10.

Let

Let us fuppofe then, that fome particular perfon, accufed of exercifing a right which interfered with the welfare of his neighbour, fhould rife up before his judges, and inform them by many authorities, that the fame right had been exercifed by a certain perfon, at fome former, but remote period of time; and having proved this, to the fatisfaction of the court, fhould fit himfelf down, in complacent expectation of a decree in his favour. Would either the judges, or auditors, think him intitled to that decree, till he had alfo gone one ftep further, and demonftrated, that *he was the perfon who had legally fucceeded to fuch right?*

But perhaps Mr. H. will contend, that the permiffion of retaining flaves *was not confined to the Jews,* but was a *general law,* extending to the whoie human race. Now, though I fhall by no means acquiefce in this conftruction of the facred books, yet let us for a moment fee what the author of the pamphlet would gain by fuch a conceffion. The refult would fimply be, that by the *unerring decifion of the great parent of the univerfe,* the ftronger nation or individual would have an *inherent right* to opprefs and reduce to fervitude, the weaker. A fuppofition as injurious to the Divine Goodnefs, as any of thofe, upon which Mr. H. has beftowed the epithets of blafphemous and prefumptuous.

Thus then you will perceive, that the ordinances of God are fometimes of a general nature, having reference to all mankind; and fometimes of a particular nature, having reference only to the people to whom they are immediately delivered. That the firft are uniformly and invariably

ably juſt and true, and that the ſecond are alſo
juſt and true, when applied to the ſubject on
which they are intended to operate; but may
become unjuſt, and improper, when applied *at
the will of man* to other purpoſes, and on other
occaſions.

As I apprehend this to be a diſtinction of great
importance in the preſent debate, I ſhall take the
trouble of giving you an illuſtration of it; by
ſhewing how differently the principles required by
Mr. H. operate upon any given ſubject, when
admitted in their full extent, and when taken
with the reſtrictions I have ventured to lay upon
them. Let this be taken from the firſt inſtance
mentioned in the pamphlet, and on which Mr. H.
lays the great weight of his cauſe, aſſerting,
" That were all other ſcriptural evidences wanting
" in favour of the Slave Trade, this decree alone
" muſt convince every impartial reader, that the
" *licitneſs* of that trade is evidently warranted by
" the written word of God."

The ſtory is that of HAGAR * the handmaid of
Sarai, who after ſhe had conceived a ſon by Abram
her maſter, fled from the ſight of her miſtreſs,
becauſe ſhe dealt hardly with her; and was
found near a fountain of water in the wilderneſs
by an angel of the Lord; who ordered her to
return to her miſtreſs, and ſubmit herſelf under
her hands, with a promiſe that the Lord would
multiply her ſeed exceedingly.

Now in making the *particular inſtance* of God's
dealings with Hagar (for which there is no doubt
he had the beſt and wiſeſt reaſons) a *general rule,*

---

* Gen. c. xvi.

B   to

to be applied on fimilar occafions, Mr. H. attempts to eftablifh a mode of proof, which, if admitted, would tear up the foundations of fociety ; — introduce and fanctify a courfe of conduct at open variance with the firft laws of truth and juftice, as derived from God ; and render it eafy to juftify any crime which the moft abandoned profligate might be induced to commit.

" Every circumftance, fays he, attending the " wretched fituation of *this poor African Slave,* " who though *legally married to her mafter,* is kept " ftill in bondage, and forced as it were out of " his houfe and fervice, in the condition fhe was " in *through hard ufage and feverity,* feems to excite " compaffion, and juftify her efcape."

Having thus allowed the apparent injuftice of Hagar's fufferings, he proceeds.

" Were Hagar's cafe that of any African Female " Slave now in the Weft Indies, and were the fame " to be tried before a jury compofed of *fome of* " *the prefent advocates for African liberty in this* " *ifland,* one might decide almoft to a certainty " in whofe favour the verdict would be given : " The flave would moft probably be declared " free ; and both mafter and miftrefs feverely " reprimanded, if not alfo condemned in a heavy " pecuniary mulct. No other verdict would be " confiftent with the principles *they fo publickly* " *avow.*—But did HAGAR obtain the fame favour- " able fentence at the impartial tribunal of God, " when fhe pleaded her caufe before the minifter " of his juftice, whom he deputed to reprefent " his perfon ? Did he approve of her conduct in " leaving her mafter's houfe, &c. ? Did he fignify " to her, that her character of Abram's wife, or

" the

" the feverity of Sarah's treatment, even in her
" actual ftate of pregnancy, emancipated her
" from her bondage, refcinded the original con-
" tract of her purchafe, or that that contract
" had been illicit, and contrary to his laws, &c.
" No. On the contrary, her conduct was con-
" demned by the reprefentative of God, who
" ordered her in his name to return to her
" miftrefs, and fubmit herfelf under her hands;
" though at the fame time he affured her *that the*
" *Lord had heard her affliction.*"

From this moft fingular comment Mr. H. immediately concludes, " that the licitnefs of the
" flave trade is evidently warranted by the written
" word of God." But before we allow the cafe
of Hagar to be a fanction for a fubfequent courfe
of conduct, of fo diffimilar a nature, let us examine
the deductions which Mr. H. in his foregoing
comment has endeavoured to draw from this
ftory, and which he muft eftablifh before it can
be of the leaft fervice to the caufe it is introduced
to fupport: Thefe evidently are,

I. That in cafe the caufe of Hagar had been
tried before a juft and impartial human tribunal,
they would have been culpable in deciding upon
it according to the known laws of juftice and
humanity.

II. That on all fubfequent occafions, where a
perfon has fuffered under the rod of oppreffion, it
is the bufinefs of a judge to fend back the fufferer
to receive further ill treatment.

III. That becaufe Hagar was ordered by an
angel to return to her miftrefs, it is lawful for
the merchants of Europe to carry on a Trade for
Slaves to the coaft of Africa.

B 2   I fhall

I fhall clofe my prefent letter with a few obfer-
vations on each of thefe deductions.

I. The Supreme Being alone can fearch the
hearts of men, and the reafons of *his immediate
determinations* are not always apparent to his
creatures, who can only form their imperfect
judgment from external circumftances.—It was
therefore no doubt confiftent with his wifdom and
juftice to direct Hagar's return. *He had power to
foften the heart of her miftrefs towards her,* and to
recompenfe her obedience as he thought good;—but
would an earthly tribunal have been therefore
excufable, in difcarding every principle of juftice,
and fending Hagar back to receive further ill
treatment? — The idea is equally wicked and
ridiculous.

II. It feems fcarcely poffible to conceive a
higher degree of prefumption, than that of ap-
plying the *particular judgments* of God to fubfequent purpofes and occafions. That a cafe *exactly
fimilar* in all points to that of Hagar has ever
fince happened, may very fairly be doubted; and
until that does really happen, the decree of the
Supreme Being *appropriated* to that cafe, can
never again be applicable. Befides, the powers
and faculties of our minds are not fufficiently
extenfive, to enable us to judge of the circumftances in all their connections, even if fuch a
cafe fhould again exift.—To reafon therefore from
this inftance, to others which evidently bear only
a *partial* or *diftant refemblance* to it, is the extreme
of arrogance; and to act in confequence of fuch
reafoning, would be the extreme of wickednefs.

III. But from what circumftances in this ftory
does Mr. H. deduce the very extraordinary conclufion,

clufion, " *That the Slave Trade, even when attended*
" *with circumftances not altogether conformable to*
" *the feelings of humanity, is effentially confiftent with*
" *the facred and inalienable rights of juftice, and has*
" *the pofitive fanction of God in its fupport ?*" What?
Becaufe the Lord, by his angel, ordered Hagar
to return to her mafter, to whom fhe was under
fome kind of obligation for fervice, whether vo-
luntary or involuntary does not appear, to whom
fhe was *legally married*, and by whom fhe was *then*
pregnant; does it by any rule of conftruction
follow, that Mr. H. or any other perfon, has *an*
inherent right, either forcibly, or by the colourable
pretext of purchafe, to feize upon an inhabitant
of *Whidah*, or *Congo*, whom *he had never before*
feen, to carry him on board a fhip, and expofe
him for feveral months to a variety of dangers;
and if he furvives, to deliver him over to a
planter, to exhauft the remainder of his days in
extreme labour, under *the immediate difcipline of*
the fcourge? — Juftice, humanity, and common
fenfe equally revolt at fuch a deduction. — But as
Mr. H. has openly difclaimed all connection with
thefe dangerous guides of human conduct, I fhall
apply my remark in a different form; and affure
him, that whenever a ftronger hand than his own
fhall hurry him on board a fhip, and confign him
to the care of an American planter for the reft of
his days, the cafe of Hagar will, according to
his own explanation of it, be as good an authority
for this proceeding, as when it was introduced to
give a fanction to the African Slave Trade,

LETTER III.

IF you will keep in view the diſtinction between a blind and ſuperſtitious admiſſion, that every fact authoriſed in the Old and New Teſtaments, is to be taken as a rule of conduct, without any conſideration of concurrent circumſtances; and the reaſonable and orthodox conſtruction of the Scriptures, which I have contended for, viz. That determinations in particular circumſtances, and under ſo peculiar a diſpenſation as that of the Jews, can be no authority for general conduct; you will hold in your hand a clue, which will ſafely guide you through all the windings and intricacies of Mr. H's *labyrinth,* and will find, that every other authority he has quoted, will, when examined by this rule, have as little weight in juſtifying the principle of the Slave Trade, as the ſtory of Abram and Hagar.

For inſtance,—the hiſtory of Joſeph's hoarding the corn, and afterwards ſelling it to the Egyptians, contains a great variety of particular circumſtances; all of them intirely different from any thing in the African Slave Trade. Joſeph had foreſeen the famine, and had prudently made a reſerve of corn during the ſeven years of plenty;

by

by which he had most probably saved the lives of the greatest part of the inhabitants; but have the merchants of Europe ever conferred a similar obligation on the natives of Africa? The purchase of this corn must have amounted to a considerable sum of money, which had been circulated amongst the Egyptians; and Joseph was therefore in some respects justified in reselling the corn, and perhaps at an advanced price. But have *such* of the natives of Africa as are reduced to slavery, ever received any kind of compensation for the deprivation of every thing dear to them? In the event it turns out that Joseph did not reduce the Egyptians to a state of actual bondage; but that he entered into a compact with them, viz. That he should give them feed to sow the land, and that they should have *four parts* of the produce, and Pharaoh the fifth part.

Not one of the inhabitants was sold to any distant country, nor ever removed out of the kingdom of Egypt; nor does it appear, that any other end was effected by this transaction, than merely the levying a tax of one-fifth of the produce throughout the kingdom; * no subsequent notice being taken in the sacred books, that the inhabitants of Egypt were held in slavery by their own kings: On the contrary, it appears that in the following reign, the Egyptians had reduced into slavery the children of Israel, and acted the part of task-masters over them.†

What then shall we think of the reasonableness and modesty of Mr. H.? who has thought it necessary to employ his time in making a calculation of the number of inhabitants at that period in Egypt; which he finds to have amounted to

* Gen. ch. xlvii. ver. 26.   † Exod. ch. i. ver. 8.

seven

feven or eight millions, and which he fuppofes is a number not unequal to all the purchafes of the kind ever made by Englifh merchants, fince the commencement of the flave trade!

After all—will it be faid, that under the light we now enjoy in the Chriftian difpenfation, the conduct of Jofeph ought to be a rule for the conduct of the governor of a country in modern times; even fuppofing it poffible the fame events fhould again come to pafs? Would it be confiftent with the very pofitive injunction of our Lord, " *Give to him that afketh thee, and from him that would borrow from thee turn not thou away?*"* The withholding the corn till the people furrendered their lands, and even their perfonal liberties, implies *a right* in Jofeph (though at that time the governor, and confequently the protector of the country) to withhold the corn, *even though the inhabitants fhould perifh for want of it.*— A pofition which may well be doubted. And, granting the ftory in the extent Mr. H. requires, where was the policy or advantage in Pharaoh being a *Slave-holder* or *Tyrant*, rather than the king of a happy and independent people?

If then the inftance of Jofeph's conduct towards the Egyptians would not in modern times, under the light of the gofpel, be a fanction for the ruler of a country under fimilar circumftances, to follow his example—how, in the name of common fenfe, can it be an authority for the *Slave Trade?* By which, without any pretence of compenfation, the inhabitants of Africa are carried away from their native country, and compelled

* Matt. ch. v. ver. 42.

to

to intenfe labour; with no further allowance than what is barely fufficient to fupport their exiftence. The inhabitants of Egypt enjoyed *four-fifths of the produce of the land*; their countrymen in modern times are not allowed *one fiftieth*. Pharaoh we are told was hard of heart. *What then fhall we think of the prefent fyftem of Slavery?*

From thefe inftances of Hagar and of Jofeph, Mr. H. informs us, he thinks he has fufficiently demonftrated that the Slave Trade has the indifputable fanction of Divine Authority, and is in exact conformity with the principles of the law of nature, as delineated in the facred writings of the word of God. But whether fuch reafoning would not difgrace any caufe, except the caufe it is intended to defend, I leave you to judge?

I now come to that part of Mr. H's work, in which he attempts to fhew, that the Slave Trade is in conformity with the principles of the *Mofaic law.* That fuch was the practice among the Ifraelites, and that fuch practice was allowed under the Mofaic inftitution, I have already admitted; but before I enter further in the difcuffion of this part of the queftion, I fhall beg leave to make one obfervation on the only hiftorical fact cited by Mr. H. under the law as an authority for flavery, viz. that of Jofhua's treatment of the inhabitants of Gibeon.

The facred writings inform us, that the land of Gibeon was given to the children of Ifrael, who were authorifed *by an exprefs revelation from God,* to deftroy all the inhabitants of the land.* For what particular crimes in the nations ad-

* Jofh. ch. i. ver. 2, 3. and ch. ix. ver. 24.

jacent

jacent to the Ifraelites thefe heavy judgments
were denounced againſt them, does not appear;
ſuch however was the power and authority with
which Joſhua was inveſted át the time the event
cited by Mr. H. took place.

But where is the revelation by which the inhabitants of Africa are delivered up to the people
of Europe? Where is the authority of the kingdom of England over that of Angola? Whence
is it derived? Who hath ever heard it aſſerted?
Or in what writings, ſacred or prophane, is it to
be found?

This circumſtance, then, which is the *foundation* and *ſole juſtification* of Joſhua's ſubſequent
conduct, being wanting in the caſe to which it
is now applied, entirely deſtroys all ſimilarity
between them.

For the Gibeonites having been abſolutely delivered up to the power of Joſhua, who was
authoriſed, and even commanded to deſtroy
them; he could, with the permiſſion of God,
change that ſeverity of treatment to a milder
puniſhment; and from ſuch change, the Gibeonites derived a great advantage, viz. the pre-
ſervation of their lives. But have the Slave-
dealers of Europe ſaved from deſtruction and
extirpation any of the nations of Africa? Have
the judgments of God been denounced againſt
thoſe people, and have ſuch judgments been
averted by the humanity or interference of the
Europeans? On the contrary, have they not,
for ages paſt, in oppoſition to the poſitive laws
of God, in open contempt of the Chriſtian religion, and without any other authority than
that of being the ſtrongeſt, deſolated and diſ-
peopled

peopled one of the moſt populous and fertile parts of the univerſe? Whether this has given them a right, equal to that of Joſhua over the Gibeonites, I leave to Mr. H. to explain. I muſt however agree with him in thinking, *that it is eaſy to conclude, whether the reducing the inno- cent as well as the guilty part of our fellow-creatures to the condition of ſlaves, or even to hereditary bon- dage or ſlavery, be in its own nature licit, or illicit, criminal, or unjuſt.* And I truſt that no per- ſon, who has candidly attended to the ſubjeċt in diſpute, can have a doubt upon the queſ- tion.

LETTER

L E T T E R IV.

I HAVE already admitted, that the practice of
slavery was permitted to the Israelites and
their immediate ancestors :—But I have at the
same time asserted, that such permission *was confined to that people only*, and was not extended
to the rest of mankind. I shall now undertake
to shew, that the practice of slavery, as allowed
to the Israelites, so far from receiving a sanction
from, was abolished by the Christian dispensation,
as being totally irreconcilable with the first principles of the religion of its divine author.

Mr. H. has endeavoured to intrench himself, by
every precaution in his power, against the attack,
which he well knew his cause was exposed to receive
from this quarter, and has stipulated, that the books
of the Old and New Testaments shall be considered
as of equal authority. But if Mr. H. be as fully
satisfied as he pretends to be, that the doctrines of
our Saviour are uniformly of the same tendency
as those of the Mosaic law, why does he so earn-
estly labour to establish a proposition, which the
greatest part of his readers will scarcely be in-
clined to grant him? Does he not appear to have
been

been aware, not only that his caufe would derive no authority from the New Teftament, but that the difpenfations of the new law, might in fome refpects interfere with and contradict thofe of the old?

That this may reafonably be prefumed to be Mr. H's true motive for endeavouring to eftablifh the equal authority of the Old and New Teftament, will appear from confidering the reafons he gives, for having been more particular in bringing the laft part of his Refearches into what he calls a central point of view, viz. " That " he has reafon to apprehend, that feveral of his " readers would be apt to imagine, that by the " eftablifhment of the Chriftian Religion the Law " of Mofes was totally abolifhed, and annulled in " every part of it; and to every intent and pur- " pofe, both typical and moral." Now it is impoffible for Mr. H. to be fo ignorant as not to know, that every fect and denomination of Chriftians admit the moral precepts of the Old Teftament, whenever they do not interfere with the purer doctrines of the Chriftian fcheme—this then could not be the true motive for his being fo particular on this head. The fact is, he hoped that by eftablifhing the equality of the Old Teftament to the New, he could with more advantage make the authorities which he pretended to find in the former, for the general juftification of flavery, militate againft the exprefs and unequivocal precepts againft it, which are contained in the latter.

Of what great importance the eftablifhment of this propofition is to Mr. H's argument, will appear from the ufe he has attempted to make of
it.

it. " From this undeniable pofition, fays he, it
" follows neceffarily, that *as the writings of both*
" *the Teftaments have the fame weight of authority,*
" effentially incapable of contradicting itfelf, in
" fupport of thofe principles and decifions en-
" acted and regiftered in their refpective records,
" concerning the intrinfic morality or immorality
" of human actions, whatever is declared in the
" one to be intrinfically good or bad, juft or
" unjuft, licit or illicit, muft inevitably be fo
" *according to the principles of the other.* If there-
" fore the Slave Trade appears, *as I truft it does,*
" from the preceding train of Scriptural Argu-
" ments, in perfect harmony with the principles
" and decifions of the word of God, regiftered
" in the facred writings of the Old Teftament,
" refpecting the intrinfic nature of that trade,
" this of courfe can bear no oppofition to, but
" muft neceffarily be in equal perfect harmony
" with the principles and decifions of the word
" of God, refpecting right and juftice,—regifter-
" ed in the facred writings of the New. This
" general but forcible argument, were it even un-
" fupported by any collateral evidences from the
" writings of the New Teftament, would be fully
" fufficient to verify my third and laft affertion
" refpecting the licitnefs of the Slave Trade, as
" perfectly conformable to the principles of the
" Chriftian difpenfation."

Thus Mr. H. has repofed the whole weight of
his argument in favour of the Slave Trade, under the Chriftian difpenfation (as unfupported by
any collateral evidence from the writings of the
" New Teftament) on this fingle propofition,
" *that the writings of both the Teftaments have the*
" *fame*

" *same weight of authority.*" I ſhall therefore firſt proceed to give the moſt indubitable evidence that *this is not the faЄt*; and that the New Teſtament *not only poſſeſſes, but has exerciſed* a controlling power over the Old, *even in points of moral conduЄt,* in conſequence of which, " This general " and forcible argument; which is itſelf ſufficient " to verify the aſſertion that the licitneſs of the " Slave Trade is perfeЄtly conformable to the " principles of the Chriſtian diſpenſation," will be found entirely groundleſs;—after which I ſhall proceed to conſider what he calls his collateral evidences derived from the New Teſtament.

After having, with ſome indecency of expreſſion, aſſerted that " God never did, nor ever could, alter by any diſpenſation whatever, thoſe eternal principles and laws, which are the very baſis and foundation of true religion; and conſequently of the religion of Chriſt," he ad- duces, as he ſays, " no leſs an authority in con- " firmation of this indiſputable doЄtrine, than the " very words of the Son of God, who in that " divine ſermon on the mount, in which he gave " his diſciples a moſt minute and circumſtantial " account of the principles and tenets of his goſ- " pel, condemned the above erroneous opinion " in the moſt explicit terms, and forbad them " even to think of it. *Think not, ſaid he, that I* " *am come to deſtroy the law or the prophets;* *I came* " *not to deſtroy, but to fulfil.*"

This being the only authority produced by Mr. H. in ſupport of his aſſertion, of the *equality of the Old and New Teſtaments,* I ſhall firſt point out, what I conceive to be the true purport of that paſſage; and ſhall afterwards produce ſuch authorities,

rities, in support of my opinion, as I think the warmest friends of Mr. H. must admit to be decisive on the point in question.

" *Think not, says our Saviour, that I am come to* " *destroy the law and the prophets; I am not come to* " *destroy, but to fulfil.*"

By which is clearly to be understood, that he came not to overthrow those first principles of morality, which are inculcated in the Old Testament, *but to improve and carry them to a higher degree of perfection;* and accordingly in the sequel of his discourse, he adverts to *many actions and modes of conduct* which were *permitted under the law,* but which he declares are *improper,* and *actually prohibits, thereby making a most essential difference between the morality of the Old Testament, and that of the New.*

Matt. ch. v. ver. 21. " Ye have heard that it " was said by them of old time, thou shalt not " kill; and whosoever shall kill, shall be in " danger of the judgment.

" 22. But I say unto you, that whosoever is " angry with his brother without a cause, shall " be in danger of the judgment, &c.

" 27. Ye have heard that it was said of old " time, thou shalt not commit adultery.

" 28. But I say unto you, that whosoever " looketh on a woman to lust after her, hath " committed adultery already with her in his " heart.

" 38. Ye have heard that it hath been said, " an eye for an eye, and a tooth for a tooth.

" 39. But I say unto you, that ye resist not " evil; but whosoever shall smite thee on thy " right cheek, turn to him the other also.

" 43. Ye

" 43. Ye have heard that it hath been faid,
" thou fhalt love thy neighbour, and hate thine
" enemy.

" 44. But I fay unto you, *Love your enemies,*
" *blefs them that curfe you, and pray for them which*
" *defpitefully ufe you and perfecute you.*"

Could any doubt remain after confidering the
foregoing paffage, as to the meaning of our Saviour's declaration, that *he came not to deftroy,* but
to fulfil, or the fuperior and controlling power of
the Chriftian difpenfation, the following explicit
declaration of the Apoftle Paul, upon the fubject,
will perhaps have as much weight as the pofitive
affertions of Mr. H. to the contrary.

Heb. ch. vii. ver. 18. " *For there is verily a*
" *difannulling of the commandment going before, for*
" *the weaknefs and unprofitablenefs thereof.*"

" 19. For *the law made nothing perfect,* but the
" bringing in of a better hope *did,* by the which
" we draw nigh unto God.

" 22. By fo much was Jefus made a furety of
" *a better Teftament.*"

Thus then it appears to demonftration, that
the Chriftian religion is not only fuperior to the
Mofaic inftitution, but that it's authority was
exerted to change or make void, or in the words
of the apoftle, " *to difannul the commandment going*
before ; and confequently all denominations of
Chriftians muft admit, that wherever the fanc-
tions and ordinances of the Old Teftament interfere with the purer doctrines and more humane
precepts of the New, they are not to be regarded
as of fufficient weight to juftify the followers of
Chrift, in the imitation of them.

Nor is it from this circumftance to be pre-
fumptuoufly inferred (as Mr. H. affects to think)

C   " That

" That God is not confiftent with himfelf; or
" that the religion of the New Teftament, in-
" ftead of being the perfection and accomplifh-
" ment, is the reproach and condemnation of the
" old law." The Mofaic inftitution was not of
general import, but was principally confined to
the Jews; and contained regulations, both of a
civil and religious nature, proper to that people,
under a Theocratic Government, but inapplicable
in many inftances to mankind in general.—Nor
was it in many refpects fo pure and perfect in its
moral precepts, as that with which mankind were
afterwards favoured. Upon this point the tefti-
mony of the Apoftle Paul, in his Epiftle to the
Galatians (who appear to have receded from the
gofpel difpenfation to the inadequate precepts of
the old law) is fo peculiarly applicable, that I
cannot avoid citing it as a full anfwer to Mr.
Harris's charge of inconfiftency in the Old and
New Teftaments.

Galatians, ch. iii. ver. 19. " *Wherefore then*
" *ferveth the law?* It was added becaufe of tranf-
" greffions, till the feed fhould come to whom
" the promife was made, and it was ordained by
" angels in the hand of a mediator.

" 21. *Is the law then againft the promifes of*
" *God? God forbid*—for if there had been a law
" given, *which could have given life*—verily *right-*
" *eoufnefs fhould have been by the law.*

" 22. But the fcripture hath concluded all
" under fin—that the promife by faith of Jefus
" Chrift might be given to them that believe.

" 23. But *before faith came* we were kept under
" the law, fhut up unto the faith, which fhould
" afterwards be revealed.

" 24. Where-

" 24. Wherefore *the law was our fchoolmafter*
" to bring us unto Chrift, that we might be juf-
" tified by faith.

" 25. *But after that faith is come we are no*
" *longer under a fchoolmafter.*"

From this paffage then it will appear, that the
daring accufation thrown out by Mr. H. that the
Supreme Being is inconfiftent with himfelf, becaufe he did not, under the Chriftian difpenfation, confirm and confine himfelf to every moral
injunction of the Old Teftament, can only be
made by *fuch perfons*, as, having for interefted purpofes attempted to eftablifh a fyftem which the
evident purport of the Scriptures cannot fupport,
have no method to hide their difgrace, but by
this direct and dreadful imputation on the facred
writings and their Divine Author.

It is alfo equally evident from the foregoing
paffages of the New Teftament, not only that
the moral prohibitions of our Saviour extended
further than the injunctions of the old law, and
rendered that conduct *unlawful*, which had before been permitted, but that fuch prohibitions
actually extended to the particular cafe in queftion, and that *all practices*, inimical to the general welfare and interefts of mankind, were from
thenceforth to be abolifhed ; for *if it be the duty
of a Chriftian not to refift evil—to love his enemies—to
blefs thofe that curfe, and pray for thofe who perfecute
him,—how can it be fuppofed that he fhall at the fame
time have an inherent right to do evil unto another—
to injure thofe who never injured him—and to deftroy
thofe, who fo far from having either perfecuted, or
curfed him, have never known that fuch a perfon was
in exiftence?*

C 2

I do

I do not conceive it neceffary to follow Mr. H. through the *tedious argument*, by which he labours to prove, that the filence of the New Teftament refpecting *the flave trade*, (fuppofing it to be filent on the fubject) is a virtual approbation of that practice. The New Teftament is totally filent on many *crimes* of the greateft magnitude, if fuch filence is to be inferred from its not containing *particular prohibitions againft them*;—but will any perfon contend that fuch crimes are lawful, becaufe no fpecific denunciations are pronounced againft them by our Saviour? Or are they not underftood to be included in thofe general prohibitions and commands, to love our neighbour as ourfelves, which compofe the fum and effence of the Chriftian religion?

But if the books of the New Teftament be filent on many particular offences, they lay down general and moft powerful precepts for the regulation of the heart and life, leaving the profeffors of Chriftianity to apply thefe precepts to particular cafes; and they who have imbibed the true fpirit of charity, breathed in the gofpel, will not find it neceffary to adopt a long train of reafoning, in order to perceive whether the *flave trade* be lawful, or not; but as foon as they underftand its nature and confequences, will feel a lively conviction, *that Chriftianity abhors the practice.*

The implied arguments of Mr. H. in favour of the flave trade, from *the exact conformity of the moral precepts of the New Teftament with thofe of the Old*, and the *filence of the New Teftament on that fpecific crime*, being thus fufficiently refuted; it may now be proper to turn to what he calls his collateral proofs from the New Teftament, or
thofe

thofe paffages which he pretends afford a pofitive fanction to the flave trade, under the new law.

This fanction he conceives he has found in two of the epiftles of Paul, viz. The 1ft of thofe to Tim. c. vi. v. 1, and that to Philemon, v. 8.

But what fhall we fay, if this flender twig, which is now the only fupport of the finking advocate for flavery, fhould defert him; and it fhould appear, from a candid and difpaffionate examination of the paffages in queftion, that the precepts of the apoftle, introduced by Mr. H. to juftify a courfe of conduct in direct oppofition to the precepts of Chriftianity, afford not the flighteft inference inimical to the general rules of goodwill and benevolence inculcated in other parts of the New Teftament?

In the paffage firft cited by Mr. H. Tim. c. iv. v. 1, the apoftle Paul exhorts " as many as are " under the yoke, to count their mafters worthy " of all honour, that the name of God and his " doctrine be not blafphemed; and that they who " have believing mafters, fhould not defpife them, " becaufe they are brethren, but rather do them " fervice, &c."—From whence he infers, " that " the primitive Chriftians were not only not for- " bidden, but *exprefsly allowed*, by the principles " of our religion, the purchafing of flaves, and " keeping their fellow creatures, nay, even their " fellow Chriftians, under the yoke of bondage or " flavery."

Now taking for granted, what perhaps may well be difputed, that the perfons fpoken of in this paffage were flaves for life,—it muft be remembered, that the great author of the Chriftian fyftem did not think proper to oppofe his authority to the

C 3 political

political arrangements which at the time of his miffion fubfifted on the face of the earth. His doctrines always inculcated fubmiffion to fuperiors, and patience under injuries; and this doctrine the apoftle applies, in the prefent inftance, to a particular clafs of perfons, to whom he thought fuch admonitions were neceffary; requiring them " to count their mafters worthy of all honour," meaning thereby, that during the continuance of their fervitude (the origin, nature, or duration of which does not appear,) they fhould perform their duty, and patiently fubmit to the fituation in which they were placed; but by no means juftifying any perfon *who held another in illegal or forcible fubjection.* The apoftle exhorts thefe fervants to account their mafters worthy of all honour, that the name of God and his doctrine be not blafphemed; *but* which Chriftian-like fubmiffion, and forbearance, *though an act of virtue in the fervant,* could by no means *juftify,* but would rather tend to aggravate, the crime of the mafter. In exact conformity to this doctrine is the precept of our Saviour, " *If any one ftrike thee on thy right cheek,* " *turn to him the other alfo.*" But will Mr. H. maintain that it is lawful to ftrike a Chriftian, becaufe his religion commands him not to refift evil? Or is it not rather the higheft aggravation, that the meek and peaceable deportment of the perfon offended, could not fecure him from infult and abufe?

The long quotation Mr. H. has made from the Epiftle of Paul to Philemon, is fo far from being a juftification of flavery, that to every perfon not perufing the fcriptures with a particular bias on his mind, it is evidently a powerful exhortation againft againſt it. The apoſtle ſends back Oneſimus to. his maſter, requeſting him to receive him, "*not as* "*a ſervant, but above a ſervant*; a *brother beloved,* " eſpecially to me, but how much more unto " thee, *both in the fleſh and in the Lord.*" Where does the apoſtle addreſs Philemon in the words ex- preſsly attributed to him by Mr. H. "*that he* "*would never attempt to deprive him of his ſlave?*" Where does he acknowledge to Philemon, "that " Oneſimus is his own brother in Chriſt, though "*ſtill his property according to the fleſh?*" Theſe paſſages ſeem to be the laſt reſort of a perſon, who, not being able to ſupport his aſſertion from the evident purport of the words, is obliged to have recourſe to *forgery and interpolation*.

Such however are the grounds upon which Mr. H. has ventured to infringe upon the poſitive commands of our Saviour, with reſpeçt to our conduçt towards each other;—but an apprehen- ſion ariſing in his mind, that theſe paſſages might, after all the pains employed in enforcing them, be inſufficient to anſwer his purpoſe, whilſt the pre- cepts of good-will given to mankind in the New Teſtament remained unimpeached—he finds it neceſſary, in the laſt place, to abridge the purport of theſe precepts, and to weaken their influence. For this purpoſe, he ſeleçts out of the many ſimi- lar paſſages which the New Teſtament affords, one which he conceives may bear a more limited ſenſe; and be explained in ſuch a manner, as not to appear inconſiſtent with his favourite eſtabliſh- ment. Whether he has been fortunate in his ſe- leçtion will appear from a ſhort inveſtigation.

Matt. c. vii. v. 12. " All things whatſoever ye " would that men ſhould do to you, do ye even

" so to them; for this is the law and the pro-
" phets."

This divine precept, delivered by Chrift to his
difciples at the conclufion of his fermon on the
mount, is fo ftrict an injunction againft every kind
of injuftice and oppreffion; expreffed in a manner
fo forcible, and prefcribing a teft of our conduct
fo eafily applied upon every occafion, that Mr. H.
was aware it could not be overlooked in this
controverfy; and he has accordingly employed
the utmoft of his fophiftry to evade its import.

After ftating the paffage, he gives the converfe
of it in the following words.

" Whatfoever things therefore we would not
" that men fhould do to us, we are not even fo to
" do to them; but no perfon whatever would
" certainly wifh that a fellow-creature fhould re-
" duce him to the condition of a flave, therefore
" no perfon whatever is to reduce a fellow-crea-
" ture to that condition."

" Here, fays he, I muft obferve, that no one
" can juftly tax me with any partiality to the
" caufe I have efpoufed; I have, I think, worded
" the argument againft it, in terms as forcible as
" the moft zealous advocate for African liberty
" could ufe; but unanfwerable as the fame may
" appear to them, it is but *a plaufible argument at*
" *beft.*

" It is an axiom in logic, that an argument
" that proves too much, proves nothing—*the*
" *above is juft fuch a one*; for by the fame manner
" of reafoning, one might equally conclude, con-
" trary to the law, and the prophets, and the doc-
" trine of the Chriftian religion, that not only
" flavery, but every other kind of fubordination
" of

" of one man to another, ought not to be fuffered
" to continue in the world. The argument, if
" conclufive in the former cafe, muft be equally
" fo in the latter. I enforce it thus :—

" *All things whatfoever*, fays our blefled Sa-
" viour, *that men fhould do to you, do ye even fo to*
" *them, for this is the law and the prophets.* What-
" foever things therefore we would not that men
" fhould do to us, we are not even fo to do to
" them ; but every perfon would naturally wifh
" not to be controlled by a fellow-creature, not
" to be *under any fubjection* to him, but to be ab-
" folute mafter of his own actions ; no perfon
" therefore ought to keep a fellow-creature under
" any control or fubjection whatever."

Surely fo manifeft a perverfion of the precepts
of Chrift, never before difgraced the prefs. *It is*
not true that every perfon would wifh *not to be con-*
trolled by a fellow-creature, nor to be under any fub-
jection to him, but to be abfolute mafter of his own
actions. Every man of common fenfe knows, that
from the conftitution of the univerfe, he is depend-
ant on, and muft neceffarily in many refpects be
controlled by others ; and none but an idiot
would wifh to be difcharged from the relative duties of life, and to be abfolute mafter of his own
actions. Nor is any fituation in life exempt from
this general law, which by an interchange of good
offices binds together the vaft fabrick of fociety—
but every man may reafonably object to his being
forcibly reduced to a ftate of flavery, and deprived of
thofe natural rights which the reft of mankind enjoy—a ftate which fo far from occafioning an interchange of good offices, gives rife on the one
hand only to pride, cruelty and injuftice ; and on
the

the other, to fear, meannefs, and hatred. It does not then by any means follow, that *becaufe* mankind have an uniform averfion to a ftate of flavery, they have *therefore* a diflike to all the other natural and juft fubordinations and dependencies of life; and Mr. H's impeachment of this precept is therefore as unfounded as all his other attempts to explain away the evident purport of the doctrines of the New Teftament.

Having found that the fenfe evidently implied in, and univerfally underftood from, thefe words, is not the true one, he gives us his own definition of it.——" Every Chriftian, fays he, is taught and
" directed to do unto others as he would be done
" unto, and by a neceffary confequence, not to do
" unto others as he would not be done unto ;—
" that is, fays he, every Chriftian is commanded
" to behave to his neighbour in whatever fitua-
" tion or circumftances in life *providence may have*
" *placed them both,* juft as he would wifh his neigh-
" bour to behave to him, in his fituation, were
" his neighbour's fituation and circumftances his
" own." Defpicable evafion! Wretched fophiftry! Shall a man, who has voluntarily and forcibly reduced another to a ftate of the moft abject mifery of which his nature is capable, impioufly affert that *providence has placed him in that fituation?* Shall he fatisfy himfelf with the plaufible pretext of acting with kindnefs towards him, whilft he has it in his power to extend to him that mercy which *in the fame fituation he would himfelf moft ardently wifh for.* As well might the midnight murderer, who holds the knife over the innocent victim of his cruelty, affert that *providence has delivered him into his hands,* and claim a merit in
putting

putting him to death with as little pain as poſſible. Surely if it be the duty of a Chriſtian to relieve thoſe who are in ſituations of diſtreſs, it is *not leſs* incumbent on him to place them in a better ſituation, as often as it lies in his power.

That the Chriſtian religion is inimical in its nature to every ſpecies of oppreſſion, and particularly to that which involves in it almoſt every other kind of guilt, is I hope already evident. But as a further confirmation of this ſentiment, it may not be improper to ſhew, what has been the general ſenſe of mankind as to the ſpirit and purport of the Chriſtian religion. So oppoſite are its precepts to the encouragement of ſlavery, that a celebrated hiſtorian,* has not ſcrupled to account for the degree of liberty, which is at preſent enjoyed throughout moſt parts of Europe, from the influence of this religion on the minds of the people.—I ſhall give you the paſſage.—

" The gentle ſpirit of the Chriſtian religion,
" together with the doctrines which it teaches
" concerning the original equality of mankind,
" as well as the impartial eye with which the Al-
" mighty regards men of every condition, and
" admits them to a participation of his benefits,
" are inconſiſtent with ſervitude; but in this,
" as in many other inſtances, *conſiderations of inte-*
" *reſt*, and *the maxims of falſe policy*, led men to a
" conduct inconſiſtent with their principles. They
" were ſo ſenſible, however, of their inconſiſten-
" cy, that to ſet their fellow Chriſtians at liberty
" from ſervitude, was deemed an act of piety

---

* Robertſon's Hiſt. Charles V. Proofs and illuſt. v. 1. note 20.

" highly

" highly meritorious, and acceptable to heaven.
" The *humane spirit of the Chriſtian religion* ſtrug-
" gled with the maxims and manners of the world,
" and *contributed more than any other circumſtance to*
" *introduce the practice of manumiſſion.*"

The ſame author furniſhes us with an authentic
document, as a proof of this fact; which, as it
proceeds from the apoſtolic chair, will have its
due weight with Mr. H. It contains the reaſons
aſſigned by Pope Gregory the Great, in the ſixth
century, for granting liberty to his ſlaves.

" Cum Redemptor noſter, totius conditor na-
" turæ, ad hoc propitiatus, humanam carnem
" voluerit aſſumere, ut divinitatis ſuæ gratia, di-
" rempto (quo tenebamur captivi) vinculo, pri-
" ſtinæ nos reſtituerit libertati; ſalubriter agitur,
" ſi homines, *quos ab initio liberos natura protulit,*
" & jus gentium jugo ſubſtituit ſervitutis, in ea
" qua nati fuerant, manumittentis beneficio, li-
" bertate reddantur."*

And the uſual tenor of the charters of manumiſſion is—*pro amore dei*—*pro remedio animæ,* &c.
clearly expreſſing the ſenſe the inhabitants of Europe have entertained, that the manumiſſion of
ſlaves was an act *in conformity to the precepts of the*
Chriſtian religion.

Were I to continue theſe authorities down to
the preſent times, and cite to Mr. H. the opinions

---

* Seeing that Jeſus Chriſt, the author of all nature, for this
expreſs purpoſe, aſſumed the fleſh, that by the favour of his
divine power (the bonds of captivity being broken) he might
reſtore us to our former liberty: We conceive it to be devout-
ly done, if, by the favour of manumiſſion, Men, whom nature originally made free, and human laws ſubjected to the
yoke of ſervitude, were again reſtored to that liberty in which
they were born.

of the many refpectable clergymen of every fect in thefe kingdoms who have oppofed this unlawful traffic; fome of them *folely and exprefsly* on the ground of its being contrary to the dictates of the Chriftian Religion, they would perhaps have little weight with him; but with the rational and difpaffionate part of mankind, they will not be without their effect; and will be no inconfiderable authority towards the deduction which I conceive I may fairly be allowed to make from the foregoing remarks, viz. THAT THE PRACTICE OF SLAVERY, AS ALLOWED AMONGST THE JEWS, WAS ABROGATED BY THE GOSPEL DISPENSATION, AND DOES NOT NOW EXIST EITHER IN THEIR IMMEDIATE DESCENDANTS, OR IN ANY OTHER PEOPLE.

If Mr. H. remains diffatisfied with a conclufion in fuch direct oppofition to the *long corollaries* at the end of his book, he muft contend, that the particular privilege granted to the Jews, and their anceftors, *is not annulled*, but yet exifts in full force. And, as I have before remarked, muft, *if fuch a privilege be hereditary*, inftitute an enquiry into their *lineal defcendants*, amongft whom I apprehend he will find fome difficulty in inrolling the inhabitants of thefe kingdoms.

But if he denies alfo this laft propofition; and afferts that the permiffion of holding others in flavery, was given indifcriminately to all mankind; I muft beg you once more to confider for a moment *the confequences and abfurdities of fuch a pofition*. If all mankind *poffefs from God*, an *inherent right to reduce into fubjection any others of their fpecies*, this right is inherent *as well in the flave as in his mafter*, who will therefore be perfectly juftified in making ufe of his utmoft exertions to
change

change situations with him; and should he succeed
in his attempt, will, *in his turn*, have " the
" positive sanction of God," for *holding by force
his former master in subjection to him.* Thus then
this universal permission or *licitness* of slavery,
contended for by the author of the pamphlet, ter-
minates in a vindication of universal oppression,—
in an assertion of the right of the stronger, at all
times to injure and oppress the weaker. In short,
in a general annihilation of all those restraints,
which Law, Reason, Religion, and Common
Sense, have hitherto imposed upon mankind.

THE END.

BOOKS Published by JAMES PHILLIPS, George-
Yard, Lombard-Street.

An ESSAY on the Treatment and Conver-
sion of African Slaves in the British Sugar Colonies. By J. RAMSAY, Vicar of Teston in Kent.
4s. Boards.

An INQUIRY into the Effects of putting a
Stop to the African Slave Trade, and of grant-
ing Liberty to the Slaves in the British Sugar
Colonies. By J. RAMSAY. 6d.

A REPLY to the Personal Invectives and
Objections contained in Two Answers, published by certain anonymous Persons, to an Essay

on

on the Treatment and Converſion of African Slaves, in the Britiſh Colonies. By JAMES RAMSAY. 2s.

A LETTER to James Tobin, Eſq. late Member of his Majeſty's Council in the Iſland of Nevis. By JAMES RAMSAY. 6d.

A LETTER from Capt. J. S. SMITH, to the Rev. Mr. HILL, on the State of the Negroe Slaves. To which are added an Introduction, and Remarks on Free Negroes. By the EDITOR. 6d.

OBJECTIONS to the Abolition of the Slave Trade, with ANSWERS. The Second Edition with Additions. By J. RAMSAY. 1s.

EXAMINATION of the Rev. Mr. HARRIS's Scriptural Reſearches on the Licitneſs of the Slave Trade. By J. RAMSAY. 6d.

An ESSAY on the Slavery and Commerce of the Human Species, particularly the African, tranſlated from a Latin Diſſertation, which was honoured with the Firſt Prize in the Univerſity of Cambridge, for the Year 1785. Second Edition with Additions, by T. CLARKSON. 3s.

An ESSAY on the Impolicy of the African Slave Trade. In Two Parts. By the Rev. T. CLARKSON. M. A. 2d Edition. 2s. 6d.

A CAUTION to Great Britain and her Colonies, in a ſhort Repreſentation of the calamitous State of the enſlaved Negroes in the Britiſh Dominions. By ANTHONY BENEZET. 6d.

THOUGHTS on the Slavery of the Negroes. 4d.

A SERIOUS ADDRESS to the Rulers of America, on the Inconſiſtency of their Conduct reſpecting Slavery. 3d.

The

The CASE of our Fellow-Creatures, the Oppreſſed Africans, reſpectfully recommended to the ſerious Conſideration of the Legiſlature of Great Britain, by the People called Quakers. 2d.

A Summary View of the SLAVE TRADE, and of the probable Conſequences of its Abolition. 2d.

A LETTER to the Treaſurer of the Society inſtituted for the Purpoſe of effecting the Abolition of the Slave Trade. From the Rev. ROBERT BOUCHER NICHOLLS, Dean of Middleham. A new Edition enlarged. 6d.

An ACCOUNT of the Slave Trade on the Coaſt of Africa, by ALEXANDER FALCONBRIDGE, late Surgeon in the African Trade. A new Edition. 9d.

WEST INDIAN ECLOGUES, dedicated to the late Lord Biſhop of Cheſter, by a Perſon who reſided ſeveral Years in the Weſt-Indies. 2s.

REMARKS on the Slave Trade, and the Slavery of the Negroes, in a Series of Letters, by Africanus. 2s. 6d.

www.ingramcontent.com/pod-product-compliance
Lightning Source LLC
Chambersburg PA
CBHW031818090426
42739CB00008B/1333